THE ORIGIN OF LIFE

CONTENTS

1 WHAT IS LIFE?

What is life? You might think that we all know what life is. We are alive. Cats and dogs, horses and cows are alive. The birds in the air, the fish in the sea—they are all alive.

All these living creatures move about. They breathe and eat. They give birth to more of their kind, and their young grow until they, too, are adults.

What about rocks? Rocks are not alive. They do not breathe; they do not eat. Rocks cannot move unless someone moves them. Although they may break and thus give rise to smaller rocks, these rock "children" do not grow larger.

A river can grow and it can move, yet a river is not alive. It does not cause its own movement and growth, but is acted upon by outside forces. A river grows wider if it is fed by smaller streams. Its water is moved by the force of gravity, which causes it to flow from higher places to lower places.

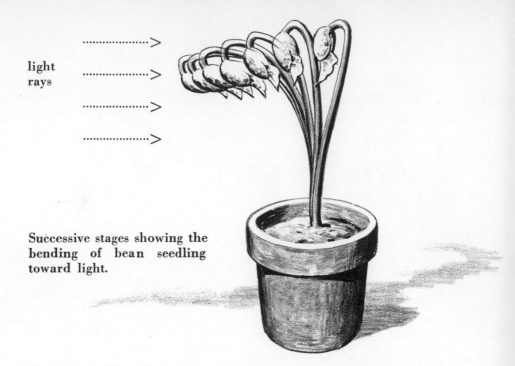

light
rays

Successive stages showing the bending of bean seedling toward light.

Are grass and trees alive? They do not seem to move or breathe, and yet they do. Plants "breathe" in oxygen from the air just as we do, and they breathe out carbon dioxide. They move, though they do so very slowly. If you sat for a while and watched a plant, you probably would not notice its movement. But if a camera were set up next to that same plant, taking one picture every half minute, you would be quite surprised at the results. By putting the pictures together to make a film, you would see that plants do move indeed. The plant that seemed so still would now be like a ballet dancer, gracefully lifting its leaves and flowers, and turning to follow the sun in its path across the sky. So plants must certainly be alive, because they move and breathe. Plants can grow and make seeds that will grow into young of their kind. Plants do not eat as animals do—they make their own food—but they use it for energy and growth, very much as we do.

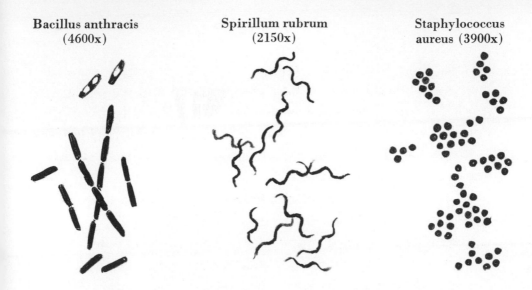

Bacillus anthracis (4600x)   Spirillum rubrum (2150x)   Staphylococcus aureus (3900x)

Three Types of Bacteria

Not all the living things in this world are big enough to see with our eyes. Some are so small that a hundred thousand of them could hide under the period at the end of this sentence. These are bacteria. The air we breathe, the vast oceans, ponds and lakes, and even the soil upon which we walk, are filled with countless numbers of bacteria and other tiny creatures. Man never suspected their existence until about three hundred years ago, a Dutchman named Anton van Leeuwenhoek peered through a microscope he had made and discovered the living world of the ultrasmall.

Though bacteria are so amazingly small, they are alive. They can breathe and they use food for energy and growth. They give rise to new bacteria like themselves. These tiny organisms sometimes change in a sudden way, and pass these changes on to their young. This kind of sudden change is called mutation.

All living things can mutate. A field of yellow corn may have a few plants whose seeds have mutated and whose ears are speckled with purple kernels. Many of the seeds from these mutated ears will grow into plants with purple-speckled ears as well. Two long-eared rabbits might have a litter in which one of the baby rabbits has very short ears, because of a mutation in one of the parents. When this baby grows up, it too may have young with very short ears.

Scientists have used mutations to help them decide whether or not something is alive. This might seem strange, since everything we have discussed has been either clearly alive or not alive, but there are "creatures" that are on the borderline of life. These are the viruses, which are even smaller than bacteria. Some scientists feel that viruses are not alive; others believe that they are.

Why should scientists disagree? Viruses do mutate, and

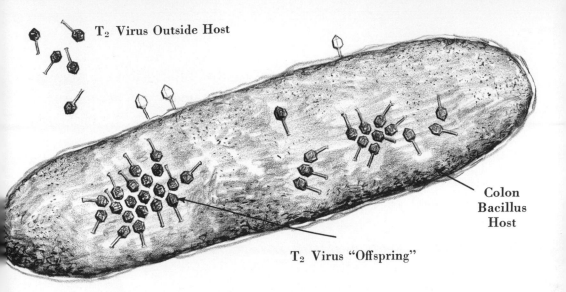

T₂ Virus Outside Host

Colon
Bacillus
Host

T₂ Virus "Offspring"

Growth of Virus Inside Bacterial Host

this is certainly something that living things do. Viruses are like living things in other ways as well. They have a definite size and shape, and their offspring have the same size and shape. For these and other reasons, many scientists say that viruses are alive.

It is a strange sort of life, however, because viruses do not grow and reproduce the way most living things do. If viruses are seen outside a living cell, they look like a crystal of salt or sugar. They do not move or breathe, and they do not seem alive at all. But once a virus is inside the cell of another living creature—just the right kind of creature for the particular virus—it becomes a center of furious activity. The virus suddenly becomes master and commands the cell it has invaded to make more viruses. Chemicals are built up and put together, energy is used, and soon there are more than a hundred new viruses, just like the original parent.

So we can see that although a virus reproduces, it does not reproduce itself; it forces the cell to make its young for it. And a virus does not really grow—it remains the same size after it has been put together by the cell that its parent had enslaved. These are the reasons why some scientists think that viruses are not really alive—for all other living things make their own young, and few have to live inside other living creatures.

There is another reason, though, and a very good one, why many scientists believe that viruses are alive. These strange creatures have within them some of the same kinds of chemicals that are found in all living things—and only in living things. Let us find out more about these "chemicals of life."

Three Varieties of Viruses

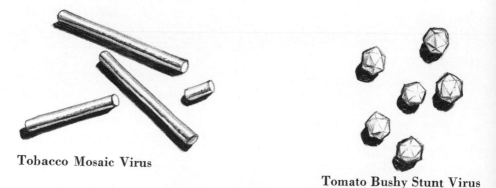

Tobacco Mosaic Virus

Tomato Bushy Stunt Virus

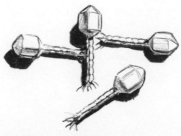

T$_4$ Bacterial Virus

2 THE CHEMICALS OF LIFE

Our whole world is made up of chemicals. The air we breathe is a mixture of chemicals, mainly oxygen and nitrogen. The water we drink is a chemical too, made up of hydrogen and oxygen (and usually small amounts of many other chemicals are dissolved in water as well). The bricks of buildings, the ground on which we walk—everything we can touch—is made up of chemicals.

Thousands of different chemicals are found in the non-living world, in rocks and sand, metal and plastics, and many other things, but there are *millions* of different chemicals that are found inside living things. Some are very simple. Many are so complicated that scientists are not sure how they are put together.

Of the many kinds of chemicals of life, three very important types are known as deoxyribonucleic acid (DNA), ribonu-

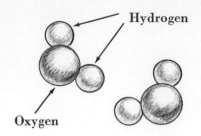

Hydrogen

Oxygen

Compare the simple arrangement of hydrogen and oxygen atoms in the water molecule, at left, to the complex structure in a very small part of a model of the DNA molecule, at the right.

cleic acid (RNA), and proteins. All living things have these three kinds of chemicals within them. These chemicals of life work together closely to help living organisms carry on the basic activities of life, and each has a special job.

The first two chemicals are called nucleic acids, and are sometimes known as the "master" chemicals of life. It is DNA that carries the complete set of blueprints for every single chemical made in a living creature. But a set of plans is not enough—there must be ways to put these plans into effect. DNA is like an architect who has the plans for a building, but an architect does not construct a building himself. He has workers to follow his plans and put the building together.

A living creature also has its "workers" to follow the plans of the architect DNA. DNA passes on its plans by making RNA. It is RNA that builds the proteins, which we can think of as the building itself, since they are the basic building blocks of life. Our hair and our nails are almost pure protein, and nearly every part of our bodies—our eyes, muscles, skin, and all our organs—are built mainly from proteins.

Some of the proteins that are made are special types called enzymes. Enzymes help the many different chemicals of the body to react—to come together or break apart or change in some way. It is the reactions of the chemicals within us that help us to live—to see, to talk, to walk, to breathe, to think, to grow. Some enzymes even help DNA and RNA to work.

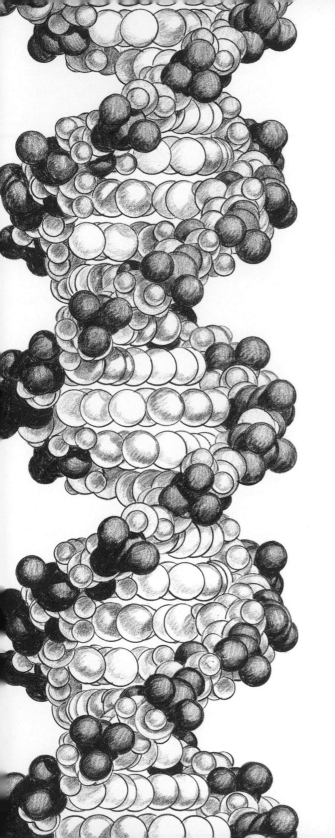

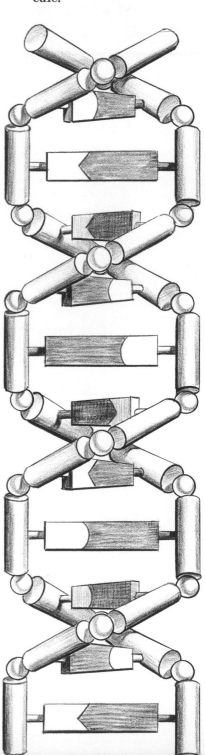

Below: A diagram of a part of the DNA molecule.

So we see that living organisms are very complex. The chemical reactions that take place in nonliving things, such as rocks and rivers, are not nearly as complicated. Is there something special about life then? How did life start? Could life come from nonliving things?

3 COULD LIFE COME FROM THE NONLIVING?

For thousands of years, people believed quite strongly that living things could spring up overnight from nonliving things. The ancient Greeks thought that if wheat were allowed to rot in the barn, it would suddenly turn into mice. They believed that mud at the bottom of a pond could give rise to frogs, and that maggots and worms could come from rotting meat.

Though these ideas seem strange to us now, the ancients were not as silly as it might seem. Their beliefs were based on what they had seen—but they had not observed carefully enough. They did see frogs come out of the mud, but they did not realize that the frogs were waking from their long winter sleep at the bottom of the pond, where they had buried themselves the autumn before. The ancients did see mice come out of rotting wheat, but they did not know that mother mice had built nests and had their young there.

Redi's Experiment

One of the first scientists who began to change people's minds about the living and the nonliving was an Italian, Francesco Redi, who lived and worked three hundred years ago. Redi wanted to see whether maggots really did come out of rotting meat. He placed pieces of meat in a few open jars. On some of the jars he placed a cover of fine gauze. Air could pass freely in and out of the small holes in the gauze, but insects could not get into the jars.

As the days passed, Redi noticed that many flies were attracted to the jars. They flew into the open jars and crawled over the meat. They crawled on the gauze that covered the other jars, too, and soon Redi noticed that the flies had laid tiny eggs on top of the gauze. In a few more days, the meat in the open jars was swarming with wormlike maggots, but there were no maggots at all on the meat in the jars covered with gauze.

Redi's discovery changed the ideas of the world. He had shown that maggots do not come from rotting meat at all. They hatch from the eggs that flies lay on the meat.

Not everyone was convinced by Redi's experiments. They found that if you filled a jar with clear broth and sealed it so that nothing could get in or out, it would still become cloudy and filled with millions and millions of bacteria. Where had they come from? A century after Redi's work, another Italian scientist, Lazzaro Spallanzani, performed a very simple experiment. He filled two bottles with broth. One of them he boiled for a long time. Then he quickly sealed both bottles, and waited. Days passed. The bottle that had not been boiled soon became cloudy, but the boiled bottle remained clear. Why was this so? Bacteria are found nearly everywhere in the world, including in the broth that Spallanzani used. By boiling the broth, the scientist had killed all the bacteria that were living in it, but in the broth that was not boiled, bacteria still lived, and grew, and multiplied.

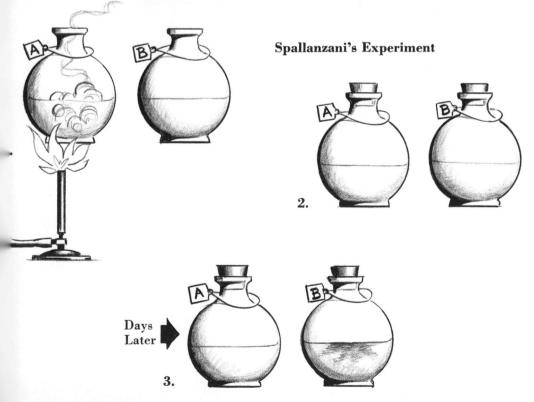

Spallanzani's Experiment

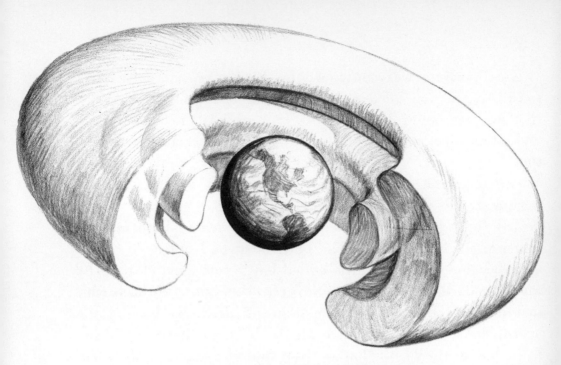

Van Allen Radiation Belt
(Partly cut away to show inner structure)

Thus Spallanzani had shown that even among creatures so small that they could not be seen without a microscope, life comes only from life.

Where then, did the *first* life in this world come from?

A few scientists believed that tiny living spores floated here from distant worlds in outer space. They thought that the spores were in a sort of deep sleep during their long trip through space, and when at last they reached Earth, they sprang into life. Now that we know of the dangerous conditions in outer space, such as the many kinds of deadly radiations, it seems unlikely that spores could survive out there for very long.

So life probably began here on Earth, a long, long time ago.

4 HOW LIFE MAY HAVE BEGUN ON EARTH

Since the days of Redi and Spallanzani, thousands of scientists have shown over and over again that life as we know it cannot arise from nonliving things. Yet the first bit of life *must* have come from the nonliving world.

Strange as it may seem, scientists now think that this is just what happened.

They believe that some time in the distant past, just the right chemicals came together to form a very simple kind of life. This life was not like the complicated forms of life that we know today. It was far more simple than even the smallest bacterium, but it was enough to start life on its way.

Scientists believe that in the beginning, when the Earth was first born, it was a huge ball of hot gases. Many many millions of years passed before a solid crust formed. No water could

possibly have existed on the hot surface of the Earth, even after the crust had formed, for the torrents of rain that fell endlessly from the thick atmosphere boiled away and turned into gases long before they reached the surface.

Little by little, the Earth cooled. At first it was too hot for any water to stay on the ground. In time, however, it was cool enough, and the rains fell—not for days, not for months, not for years—but for centuries, and the world became covered with water.

The Earth at that time was often rocked by explosions so gigantic and violent that a thousand hydrogen bombs, exploded all together, could not compare with them. Mountains rose up out of the Earth and towered over the oceans. In time, these

first mountains were worn away by the rains and new mountains were thrust up.

Lightning flashed through the atmosphere, which was probably very different from the one Earth has now. Now our atmosphere is mostly nitrogen and oxygen, with small amounts of carbon dioxide and water vapors. By examining the rocks of the Earth's crust and looking at the atmospheres of other planets through powerful telescopes and spectroscopes, scientists have discovered that when the Earth was young, its atmosphere was probably filled with the gases methane, ammonia, nitrogen, hydrogen, and water vapor, along with small amounts of carbon dioxide and sulfur compounds. There was no free oxygen at all.

For millions and millions of years, light from the Sun and radiations from space streamed down on the strange atmosphere of the ancient Earth. With the energy from these radiations and electricity from the crackling lightning, the gases in the atmosphere reacted with one another. More complicated chemicals were formed in the atmosphere and drifted down, to dissolve in the warm seas below. The seas became like a giant soup of chemicals, which grew thicker as time passed.

These countless numbers of chemicals in the ocean were constantly bumping into one another. Sometimes they stuck together, forming something new. Or perhaps they bumped into one another and then parted, each having changed the other in some way. These were chemical reactions.

Sometimes a number of chemicals tended to stay together in groups. Sometimes these groups picked up new chemicals from the soupy seas and grew in size, but this was not yet life as we know it.

Some of these groups contained nucleic acids, rather like the DNA and RNA in our present world. Some also contained proteins as well.

Somehow, at some time—or more likely at many different times—in the long-ago past, a strange and wonderful thing happened. One of these nucleic acids, perhaps with the aid of a protein which acted as an enzyme, was able to reproduce itself. Now there were two of this remarkable group of chemicals. The two floated their separate ways, each gathering in new chemicals from the soupy seas. In a short while, each became two, and the two became four, and the four became eight. Soon the seas were filled with many of these "pre-life" forms—or were these the beginnings of life?

Ultraviolet rays from the Sun and cosmic rays from outer space continued to stream down upon the Earth. Often a cosmic ray or ultraviolet ray struck one of the "pre-life" forms. Every now and then, this caused a change in the nucleic acid—a mutation. Most of the time, the changes were not very important. Or perhaps they even hurt the tiny form of "pre-life" and made it less able to survive in the soupy seas. Once in a while, the change was helpful and made the small "pre-life" form a bit better able to survive. Perhaps it could reproduce more rapidly. Perhaps it was able to capture new chemicals better than its neighbors. Perhaps it formed a thicker covering about itself to protect the chemicals inside.

Life as we know it did not suddenly appear on Earth. Instead, it came one small step at a time. Perhaps it took millions of years, perhaps tens of millions. We do not know. And even if we had been there to watch, who could say "This was life," or "This was not"? As we have seen, there is a borderline of life that is not sharp at all. Some of the creatures that we know today, such as viruses, seem to be "living" at times and "non-living" at other times.

Finally a creature came to be, which all would recognize as life. It could live by itself, make its own food—or gobble it down from the seas around it—and reproduce itself.

Is this the way life actually began on Earth? No one can say for sure, but scientists do know from their experiments in the laboratory that this is the way it *could* have happened.

5 EXPERIMENTS ON THE ORIGIN OF LIFE

The amazing idea that the first living creatures actually arose from nonliving chemicals was presented by a Russian scientist, A. I. Oparin, in 1924. The scientists of the world were fascinated by this idea and wondered if this is what really happened. How could this be proven? There certainly were no people around before there was life! And so we have no eyewitness accounts at all of how life actually began.

In the 1950s, some scientists thought of ways to test ideas on the origin of life right in the laboratory. Two American researchers, Harold Urey and Stanley Miller, recreated in their laboratory at the University of Chicago what was thought to have been the atmosphere of the ancient Earth. For nearly a week they sent electric sparks through this atmosphere. At the end of this time, the experimenters were surprised to find some of the simple chemicals of life. Among them were amino acids—the building blocks from which proteins are made.

28

Scientists throughout the world became very excited at this discovery. They not only repeated Miller and Urey's experiments, but they made changes of their own. One scientist added a little phosphate—the kind one finds in the rocks of the Earth—and the amino acids that were formed joined to each other to form larger compounds. According to all the chemical tests, these were proteins. But were they like the proteins made by living things? The scientist fed them to bacteria, who gobbled them as though they were real proteins.

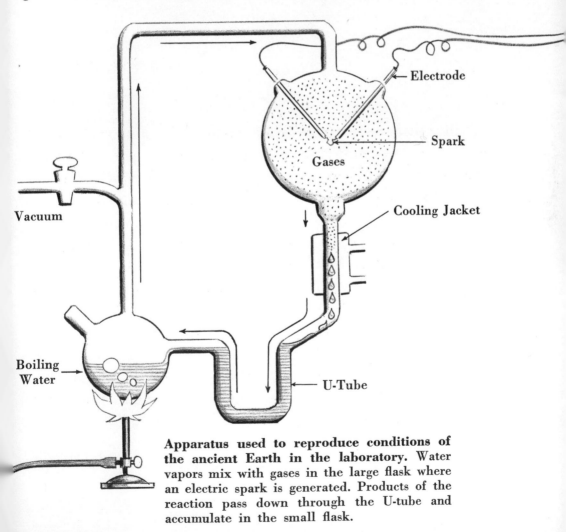

Apparatus used to reproduce conditions of the ancient Earth in the laboratory. Water vapors mix with gases in the large flask where an electric spark is generated. Products of the reaction pass down through the U-tube and accumulate in the small flask.

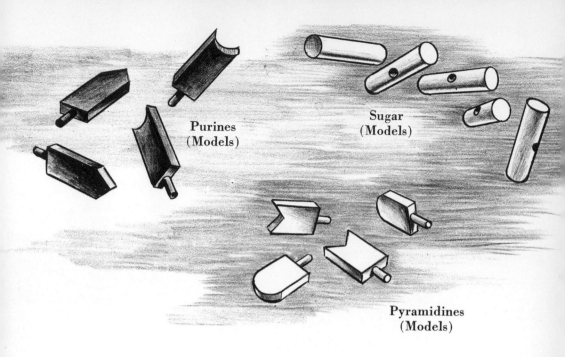

Purines
(Models)

Sugar
(Models)

Pyramidines
(Models)

Still other researchers made chemical compounds called purines and pyrimidines, and others made sugars—all in the same kind of atmosphere, with the same chemicals, that are believed to have existed on Earth long ago. When they joined these purines, pyrimidines, and sugars with phosphates, they were able to make compounds called nucleotides. These are the building blocks from which nucleic acids—DNA and RNA—are made, just as amino acids are the building blocks of proteins.

Many other chemicals of life were made also, including porphyrins, which are related to hemoglobin, the red pigment in our blood, and to chlorophyll, the green pigment in plants. These porphyrins can take in energy from sunlight; the energy that they hold can later be used in many different chemical reactions.

Another complicated chemical made in the laboratory from

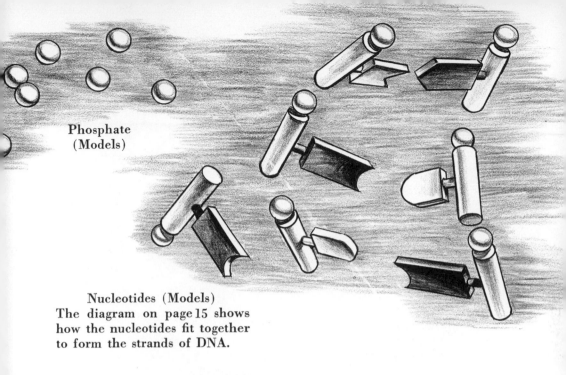

Phosphate
(Models)

Nucleotides (Models)
The diagram on page 15 shows
how the nucleotides fit together
to form the strands of DNA.

simple compounds that could have been found on the ancient Earth was adenosine triphosphate, or ATP. This is a very important chemical of life, for it is used as a storehouse of energy by almost all living things. Without ATP, life as we know it could not exist.

So the scientists showed in their laboratories that just about all the chemicals needed for life could indeed have been formed from the nonliving chemicals in the strange atmosphere and warm, soupy seas of the ancient Earth.

An important question still remained. These chemicals could have been formed, but could they have come together to produce life?

The Russian researcher A. I. Oparin tried a new experiment. He mixed solutions of two substances—gelatin and gum arabic—together, and tiny droplets formed. A mixture of these droplets with enymes helped chemicals to react much more

31

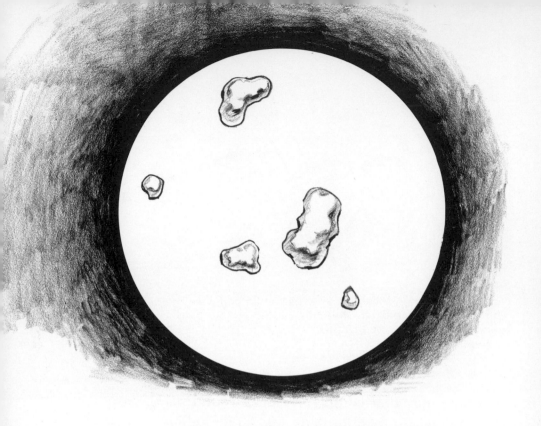

**Microscopic View of Oparin's Droplets
of Gelatin and Gum Arabic**

quickly than they did when the enzymes were just dissolved in water, with no droplets present. This is just what happens in living cells.

Oparin's droplets were the beginning of an answer. But in many ways they were not like living cells at all, for his droplets were of many different sizes and shapes, and they easily broke apart. Even more important, Oparin's droplets of gelatin and gum arabic were made from chemicals that had been produced by living things. Could *non*living chemicals come together to form such droplets?

32

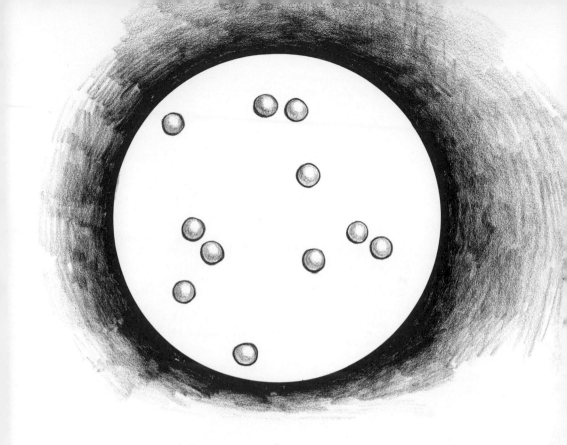

Fox's Microspheres

American researchers, including Sidney Fox at the University of Miami, went on working. They took the amino acids that had been made in an atmosphere like that of the ancient Earth, heated them, and formed proteins. Then they added water, as could have occurred on the ancient Earth when it rained, or when the tides of the ocean lapped at volcanic shores, and an amazing thing happened. The proteins formed tiny balls. These balls were rather like Oparin's droplets, but there was an important difference: they were all about the same size—about the size of bacteria cells.

The scientists looked at their tiny protein balls under powerful microscopes. They looked rather like bacteria. They had a thickened coat about them, as bacteria do. And this coat, like that of a bacterium, seemed able to let certain chemicals pass through while it stopped others.

More tests were run. It was found that the proteins of the tiny balls, or microspheres as they are called, acted like enzymes. Then it was discovered that these protein microspheres could reproduce! If they were kept in the solution in which they were originally formed for a week or so, they began to grow small buds.

The researchers grew excited, because there are some living

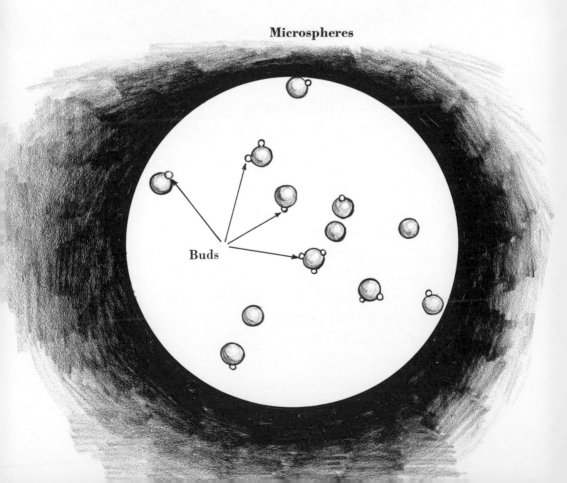

Microspheres

Buds

cells, such as yeasts and certain bacteria, which reproduce by forming buds. What would happen if the buds were separated from their "parent" microspheres?

It turned out to be easy to separate the buds—an electric shock or even a sudden bump would do it. These buds were then left quietly in the solution.

They began to grow. They grew and grew until they reached the size of their parents. Then they stopped growing. The researchers left the new "daughter" microspheres in the solution, and soon these little protein balls began to form buds of their own! A new generation of protein microspheres was being "born."

Yeast Cells

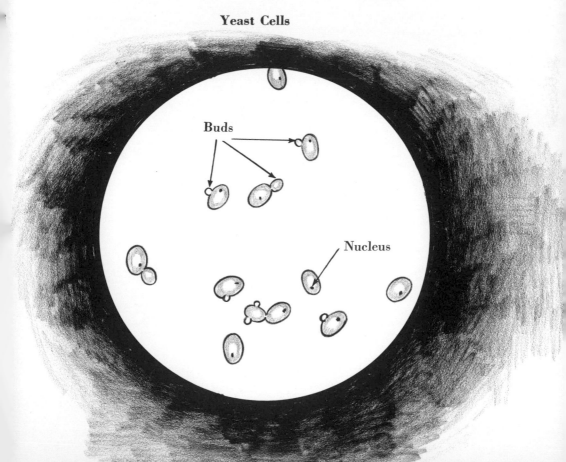

The little protein microspheres, formed entirely from non-living chemicals, seem almost like life. This is not life as we know it, for they do not contain nucleic acids. But scientists believe that in the seas of the ancient Earth, such proteins microspheres could have gathered together nucleotides—the building blocks of the nucleic acids—and thus could have held all the chemicals together that were necessary to form the first cells.

6 THE EVOLUTION OF LIFE ON EARTH

The first truly living organisms on Earth were single-celled creatures. These creatures must have been able to live without oxygen, because there was no oxygen in the atmosphere, nor any dissolved in the sea. Mutations followed mutations, and both the life forms of the Earth, and the Earth itself, began to change.

Some of these changes must have allowed early life forms to capture energy from the sunlight that shone on the Earth, and use this energy to make food for themselves. This process is called photosynthesis. As the new photosynthetic creatures multiplied and spread through all the seas of the world, they began to change the oceans and atmosphere. An important "waste product" of photosynthesis is oxygen, and the oxygen that these organisms made was passed into the waters of the world, and then into the atmosphere. For millions of years, the atmosphere was being filled with oxygen. As more and more mutations occurred, some creatures appeared which were able to use this newly freed oxygen to burn food and to provide energy for the activities of life.

At this point, only one-celled creatures filled the waters of the world. Some made their own food; others fed upon the chemicals dissolved in the waters. As more and more living creatures grew and multiplied, however, the atmosphere changed. Fewer new chemicals were formed and drifted down into the seas, and the simple chemical foods dissolved in the oceans became scarce. New life forms arose, which fed upon other living creatures—and the first animals were born.

Some primitive microscopic one-celled creatures, capable of manufacturing their own food, being devoured by primitive one-celled animals.

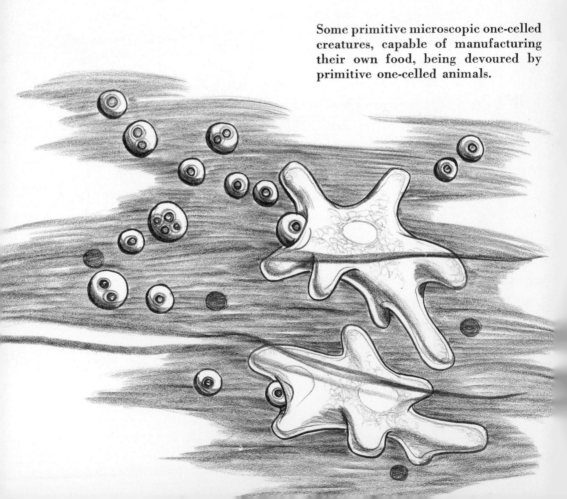

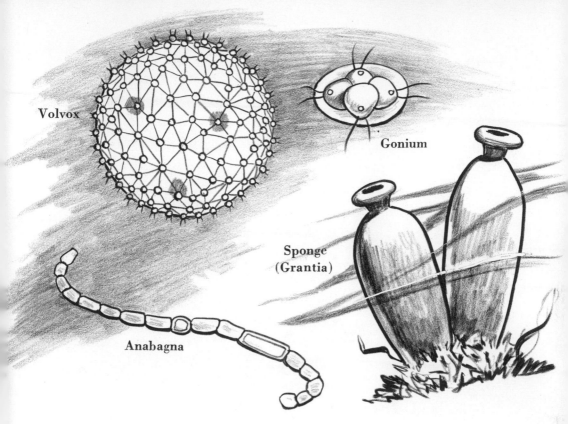

Volvox

Gonium

Sponge
(Grantia)

Anabagna

Some surviving types of cell colonies

An ever-changing variety of new life forms was appearing. In time, most would disappear and never again be seen on Earth. Their places were taken by others who could reproduce faster, eat better, or were in some other way better fit to survive. Cells came to live together, first in small groups, and then in larger and larger colonies. In some groups, different cells came to do different tasks—some defended the group; others captured or made food; still others reproduced. The new many-celled creatures often got along better than their one-celled neighbors. The fittest survived, and those that were not fit disappeared from the Earth.

This was a long process. More than two *billion* years went by from the beginnings of life until many-celled creatures that we would recognize appeared. As the evolution of life went on, sponges appeared, and jellyfish, corals, and other creatures that dwell quietly in the sea. Soon the ocean bottoms swarmed with crabs and snails and worms of many kinds. Shrimplike and spiderlike creatures swam through the waters. No fish had yet appeared, and though the oceans swarmed with life, the lands were still bare: there were not yet any plants or animals on the lands of the Earth.

The Earth itself was not quiet. While this long succession of life forms was developing, there were great upheavals. New mountains were thrust up, and other lands sank beneath the sea. Sometimes the Earth was hot, and sometimes glaciers, mountains of ice, moved down from the poles to cover much of the land. These great changes helped to shape the evolving patterns of life, for only the life forms that were able to adapt to the Earth's changing conditions survived. The others disappeared.

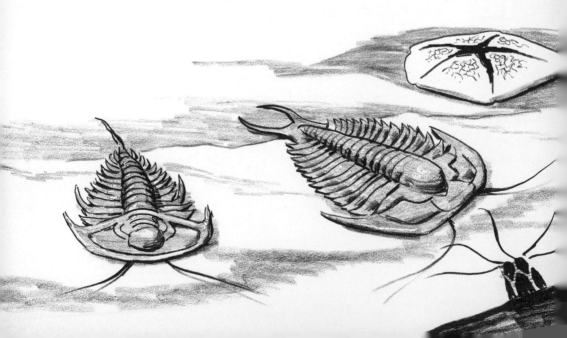

Millions of years went by, and fish appeared and spread throughout the oceans of the world. At the same time, the plants of the sea began to invade the land. Later, animals that looked like scorpions and salamanders began to venture onto the land.

Life on the land was very different and far more difficult than life in the sea. Plants and animals in the seas were kept moist by the water that surrounded them, but those that came to live upon the land could not survive unless they had some

Some fish that populated the oceans 400 million years ago.

Early Amphibious Creatures

way to keep from drying out. Another problem that the plants and animals faced was that of support for their weight. A water plant or animal can float effortlessly, for the water itself helps to hold the organism up. On land, all the weight of the body is pulled down by gravity. Air does not help to support it. On land, too, there are great temperature changes, from day to day and from season to season. In the seas the temperature changes are much smaller and take place much more slowly.

43

These were serious problems indeed, but there were advantages to life on land. Here was a whole new world, free from the crowding and competition of the swarms of life in the sea. And so when mutations occurred that permitted organisms to adapt to the harsher conditions of the land, they left the sea, and survived and multiplied on land. In time there were more and more mutations, which allowed them to continue their adaptations to land living.

The first land plants were tiny forms, but in time there were larger and larger plants able to support themselves. Great forests began to cover the lands. The first land animals had to stay close to the water, to keep their bodies moist and lay their eggs there when it was time to mate. Eventually there were newer and newer forms, some of which were even able to live in deserts. Insects, reptiles, birds, and mammals appeared. At last, flowering plants and even manlike animals developed.

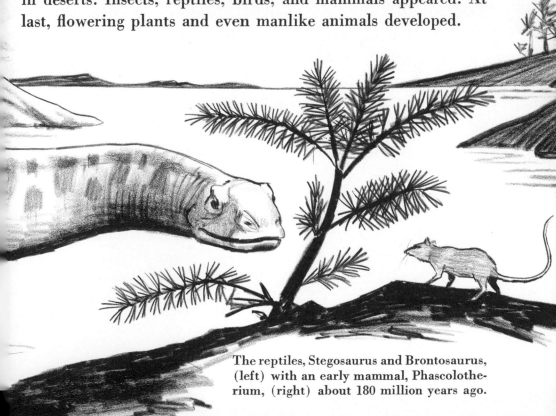

The reptiles, Stegosaurus and Brontosaurus, (left) with an early mammal, Phascolotherium, (right) about 180 million years ago.

Man himself appeared on the Earth about two million years ago. He was shaped by the same sort of forces and conditions that molded his ancestors—from the microscopic single-celled life forms that first appeared on Earth billions of years ago, to the cold-blooded animals that swarmed in the seas and their descendants that crawled out onto the land, to the first tiny warm-blooded mammals that bore their young alive, and to the apelike almost-men, whose descendants, at last, were men.

The story of evolution is not yet ended. The forces of our Earth are always acting upon the animals and plants of the world, and these living organisms are interacting with one another. Changes are still going on. Life forms adapt to our ever-changing world, and those which cannot adapt die and disappear. Man himself has had a greater influence upon our world than any other creature before him. Each year he cuts away forests and drains swamps and builds giant dams. Scientists believe that with his burning of fuels, man is changing the climate of our planet. As man gains more and more knowledge, his ability to change the Earth and control the living things upon it is increasing. Only time can tell what the future story of evolution will be.

INDEX